I Need a kidney: Now what?

I Need a kidney: Now what?

Life Lessons From A Two-Time Kidney Transplant Recipient

LINDA NELSON

ISBN-13: 9781983723322
ISBN-10: 1983723320
Library of Congress Control Number: 2018900387
CreateSpace Independent Publishing Platform
North Charleston, South Carolina

Dedication

I would like to dedicate this book to my parents, Cliff and Betty Fredell, who taught me so many of the lessons in this book. Because of you my glass looks half full.

In addition, I would like to thank from the bottom of my kidney, all of those living and deceased, who have donated the gift of life.

You are my heroes!

My heroes!

Foreword

I'm a sucker for a story with a happy ending. Always have been. But never in my dizziest daydreams did I imagine I'd get to be part of one, and certainly not the story of a life saved.

In so many of the great stories in literature there is an inevitability to the way that the storyline unfolds, and that is certainly true in this story. By the time that I learned that my friend, Linda Nelson, needed a kidney it just seemed obvious, inevitable, that I should be a part of her story. And as you'll see as you read Linda's story, like all great stories the plot line from beginning to happy ending is anything but straight.

It would be an understatement to say that Linda has been through a lot in her life, but you'd never know it by meeting her. Always smiling, constantly optimistic, forever ready with a word of encouragement for others, Linda exudes positivity. One of the many life-lessons you'll learn in these pages is how to face adversity with a smile.

And perhaps as you pick up this story that's exactly what you need – some encouragement. I'm imagining that many of the people who peruse these pages are somewhere in their own story of kidney disease of one kind or another. It's an all-too-familiar story with over 80,000 people on the waiting list for a transplant. If you're one of them, it's my prayer that this story will bring you hope and the strength you need to refuse to give up. Miracles do happen, and you never know who is feeling the "nudge" to be a donor for you.

Or perhaps you're thinking about being a donor. Good for you! I can't encourage you strongly enough to pursue the possibility. I'd love to welcome you into the "One Kidney Club" whose members get to doze off each night knowing that they've made a real difference in someone's life. The experience of being a live kidney donor has taught me the great truth that it really is better to give than to receive.

I hope you enjoy Linda's story. More importantly, I hope that in these pages you'll discover just what you need to live your own story, all the way to its happy ending.

Jeff Marian

One

Now What

Our wedding May 1994

It was 1995 and I had just turned 40 years old and had gone in for my annual physical. The doctor mailed my lab results home with a red circle around the creatinine level, calling my attention to the fact that it was a little high. After checking my blood-screening pamphlet, I realized the creatinine level was an indicator for kidney problems. Most people are born with two kidneys the size of a large fist, on either side of their spine in the back. They are designed to remove waste from the blood and keep the body's fluid levels balanced. If the kidneys don't work, the body doesn't work. My chest began to tighten and fear began to creep up my spine.

My dad and my mom's uncle were two of the first dialysis patients in the country. I called my doctor back immediately. He was not too concerned, thinking I was a little dehydrated the day of the blood test, but when I explained kidney disease ran in my family he decided to retest. **(LIFE LESSON: YOU ARE YOUR OWN BEST ADVOCATE.)**

After a couple of weeks of additional abnormal test results I was referred to a kidney specialist. My new nephrologist, Dr. Somerville, did more testing, scans, and eventually a kidney biopsy. It was determined I was in kidney failure and would eventually need a transplant. I froze. There were no words.

Dr. Somerville explained that the biopsy showed scar tissue in my kidneys and the specific kidney disease I was blighted with could not be determined. The fact was, it did not really matter, as the outcome was the same. He would monitor and care for me until my kidneys deteriorated to the point of transplant. The next six years were regimented with labs and doctor appointments. I must say waiting for my kidneys to fail was not an easy task. I did not feel sick, so the danger became being in denial about the fact that I was. The other danger was being so consumed by my illness that it would get in the way of living my life! I had to learn to walk the fine line between knowing the sickness was real without allowing it to become my sole reality. **(LIFE LESSON: LIVE IN THE PRESENT.)**

During this time I had a difficult time going into my doctor appointments knowing my labs would only get worse as the months and years went along. Dr. Somerville experimented with putting me on a low protein diet in hopes of extending the life of my natural kidneys. I hated that! I was hungry all the time and I gained weight. At least I felt like we were "doing" something for the moment. Eventually it was determined the low protein diet did not make much of a difference.

Patience is not one of my strong suits and I remember asking Dr. Somerville what we were waiting for. I knew my kidneys were failing and there was no stopping them. I thought getting a new kidney was like replacing a broken transmission in my car. I just wanted to get the new part put in so I could be fixed and move on. I had no idea at the time that it was impossible to ever be really fixed. It was more like being told, " We have a way to get your car back on the road, but the transmission is from another year, make, and model of car so we will have to adjust, alter, and rework it to make it fit. In addition, the roads may be bumpy, and as a result, the car will need frequent service checks."

As expected, the day arrived when Dr. Somerville told me my kidneys had deteriorated to the point that my natural kidneys were not going to last much longer and I would need a new one soon. Tears ran down my face as the reality hit me. My kidneys were almost gone. I had understood this day would be coming for almost six years. I had even wished it would come faster so I could get it over with. Yet, when the day arrived I was not only sad but also scared to death. Now what!?!?

Questions flooded my brain. I had no idea how to do this! Dr. Somerville referred me to Hennepin County Medical Center in Minneapolis (HCMC), the same hospital my dad had been at several decades ago. He could have referred me to any of the highly acclaimed transplant centers in Minnesota yet he sent me to the one where he felt I would get the most individual care. I was not a number; I was Linda, mother of Megan and Rachel, stepmom to Mark, Paul, and John, wife to Tom, and daughter of Betty and Cliff. Wait, daughter of Cliff! I remembered Dad telling me that if anything that he had gone through in his kidney disease journey could help someone else it would all be worth it. Little did we know that one day it would be ME! I felt like I was going home. **(LIFE LESSON: REMEMBER WHOSE YOU ARE AND WHERE YOU CAME FROM.)**

Two

Dad

I was 10 years old when my 36-year-old father was diagnosed with kidney failure. He had gone in for a required physical when he became an officer for Northwestern National Bank. Transplants were new in 1965 and the success rate was not very high. My dad had no other living siblings and his parents had both passed away so having a family member donate was not an option. A huge problem was at hand. Coincidentally, my mom's uncle was diagnosed with kidney failure a few months before my dad. He informed my folks about the new machine, called a hemodialysis machine, brought to Minneapolis from Seattle, Washington by Dr. Fred Shapiro. Dr. Shapiro pioneered the dialysis program in Minnesota at Hennepin County General Hospital.

The hemodialysis machine miraculously was able to remove a patient's blood, cleanse it from the toxins the sick kidneys were unable to purify, and return it to patient's body purified. It was a new process but the odds of surviving on a machine were better than a transplant, given my father's situation.

Qualifying for the program was quite rigorous. Because my dad was young, healthy, had four young children, and worked a full -time job with good health insurance, he was selected to become a dialysis patient.

I Need a kidney: Now what?

The Minneapolis Star and Tribune newspaper publicized the new hemo-dialysis machine on the front page with a picture of my father lying in a hospital bed grinning his big "Michael Strahan" smile under the head-line: "Who shall live and who must die." Doctors had the daunting task of having to select candidates who had the greatest chance of success. The line was long and we were fortunate Dad was chosen to live.

Dad's life was reorganized to receive dialysis treatments downtown Minneapolis at General Hospital (now HCMC) three times a week. He walked to the hospital after work Monday and spent ten hours hooked up to the dialysis machine, which meant he stayed overnight. In the morning, he would get ready for work, walk back, spend the day at the bank, and ride the bus home that evening. He did the same Wednesday and Friday nights. Saturday morning Mom would drive downtown to pick him up.

Dad's schedule affected much of the entire family's schedule as well. Family vacations were nearly impossible with Dad's dialysis schedule, but he was creative. Soon an above-ground pool was installed in our back-yard. Then our pastor, Pastor Johns, heard that saunas were good for dial-ysis patients because they allowed toxins the kidneys could not dispose of to be perspired out in between dialysis runs. Pastor Johns arranged for a number of church members to surprise Dad by building a sauna in our basement. With the addition of a pool and a sauna, Dad had sur-prised us with a family vacationland in our backyard. (**LIFE LESSON: GET CREATIVE, WHERE THERE IS A WILL, THERE'S A WAY.**)

One of the few family vacations we were able to experience apart from our back yard oasis was a week at family church camp. We packed up the station wagon and drove 140 miles or so to the camp. Mom and Dad had to drive back to Minneapolis twice that week for Dad's dialysis runs, but the other families kept an eye on us kids. Since there were two families per cabin, we couldn't get into too much trouble when Mom and Dad were gone for the night.

Another memory I have is being invited to a weekend getaway at Uncle Ernest and Aunt Helen's cabin a couple of hours away from home. I recall Dad and Ernest cleaning their cannulas together at the table and talking about the "club." They belonged to a very elite group, but to us it was our norm. The cannula was a U-shaped plastic tube inserted into a vein and artery to access the machine. They covered it with gauze and an ace bandage. We knew someone was part of the club when we saw the bandage on their arm. Dad's cannula burst open like Old Faithful more than once! He would quickly grab a towel and apply pressure, as Mom rushed him to the hospital so he wouldn't bleed to death.

Dialysis patients frequently suffered infections. About three years into dialysis Dad was given a heavy-duty antibiotic for one of the life-threatening infections he had, and as a result he lost his hearing. I was in 7th grade and practicing for my first solo in choir. My heart broke when we realized he could never hear me sing again.

Yet Dad came to every one of my concerts, with the exception of my senior voice recital in college. He had had a heart attack the week before. I was so worried that I immediately drove from Gustavus Adolphus College to the hospital. I brought my recital program with me to show him. His response to me was he would take the program out at the exact time my recital began miles away and follow along. **(LIFE LESSON: YOU DO NOT HAVE TO BE THERE TO BE THERE.**)

After many years of Dad's dialysis routine, his health insurance ran out. He had to stay out of the hospital for 90 days before it could rein-state. Dr. Shapiro arranged to send a dialysis machine to our home so Dad could continue his treatments. By this time, the machine was some-what the size and shape of a washing machine and the time a patient needed to be hooked up to it had decreased from ten hours to six hours.

When I was in grade school I recall making a model of the older version of the hemodialysis machine for my science fair project. I made it out of a shoebox, with plastic cellophane layers inside the box and plastic tubing that Dad scrounged up from the hospital. This contrap-tion won me a ribbon, but more importantly, it was saving my dad's life.

Somehow, the new washing machine version dialysis machine was manipulated through the door of my parents' bedroom and hoses were stretched across the room to the attached bathroom. This enabled all the fluids to drain when needed. Dad was able to lay in the comfort of his own bed! My sister Sue especially liked to play nurse. She practiced taking his blood pressure and temperature. While Dad's blood was being cleansed, my brother, in particular, played football in the yard with the technicians and the nurse pierced my sister Carrie's ears. I was too chicken!

Dad's insurance reinstated in ninety days, which was way too fast for all of us.

Our family life was busy for my mom with four young children and a sick husband. Mom modeled being a healthy caretaker for my siblings and myself. She was somehow able to create normalcy while never knowing what the day would bring with my father's health. I remember planning to go to a family reunion when Dad got sick at the last moment. Mom arranged for a relative to pick up my siblings and myself and off we went. She stayed home with Dad. Going with the flow was important not only for the sick family member, but for the whole family. When the sick person feels good, capitalize on it! (**LIFE LESSON: SPONTANIETY IS A GOOD THING.**)

I would be remiss not to mention one of the greatest gifts I learned from my father: have a sense of humor. Dad played many tricks on the nurses during his long dialysis runs. One time he got a hold of a big plastic pill that was about the size of a football. He would call a nurse over to let them know that for some reason he wasn't able to take his pill. Surprise, out came the gigantic plastic version! When he was asked what he would like to have for dinner during his run, pheasant under glass or a T-bone steak were his top choices, with a martini. I know his jokes expedited the night for those taking care of him as well. (**LIFE LESSON: FIND A WAY TO LAUGH.**)

The greatest gifts my parents shared with all of us were the gifts of faith and gratitude. No matter what happened in life they knew God would take care of them. Every morning I could hear Dad whisper (Dad's non-hearing whisper was louder than he thought) "THANK THE LORD FOR ANOTHER DAY." No matter what the day would bring, they tackled it together with gratitude. (**LIFE LESSON: LIVE LIFE WITH GRATITUDE.**)

Backyard vacation in our pool

Who Shall Live and Who Must Die

Three

DEATH

My brother, sisters, and I learned at a very early age that death was part of life. Many of Dad's dialysis friends had passed away over the years, but it was extremely hard when Uncle Ernest died in 1971 after 6 years together on dialysis. He was Dad's confidant, friend, and relative. I remember my dad crying when we got the call. Death had hit a little too close to home for all of us. Dad and Ernest lived life knowing they were cheating death every day. In many ways, I believe we had become immune to that. Yes, death happens to everyone someday but not to my dad. He had escaped it more than once. One of our neighbors told Mom she had had her husband's black suit out many times thinking Dad was not going to make it. We became so used to living with the possibility of death but when it happened it was almost a shock.

Dad lived nearly 10 years after Ernest died. I realized the last week of Dad's life, that in spite of his illness, he had made an impact on so many people! The hospital staff began to trickle in to say their goodbyes to Dad. The one I remember most was Dr. Shapiro, Dad's doctor for nearly 17 years. He no longer worked directly with patients but wanted to make sure he said good-bye to one of his first who was also his friend. He quietly told the staff to make sure Cliff was comfortable and had everything he needed. As he looked into the eyes of our family, he saw the faces of Cliff's now grown children. He could do nothing else.

I arrived at the hospital one of his last afternoons and a nurse told me Dad had been calling my name. I sat on his bed, and although I knew he was in a coma and couldn't hear, I told him it was ok to let go. He had fought to raise his family for nearly 17 years. He saw all of his children through elementary school, junior high, high school, senior high, and half of us through college. I telepathically told him we were ok and he could let go. We would be fine. He had done well.

Dad died on May Day, 1982 at HCMC under the care of a stellar staff that had become not only his family but also ours. **(LIFE LESSON: DEATH IS A PART OF LIFE.)**

Four

HCMC Transplant Center, Here I Come

S cience and research had made huge progress in the transplant arena since the early 1960s and great advancements in anti-rejection medications since my fathers' passing in 1982. Dad had been called only one time for a possible deceased donor match in the nearly 17 years he lived on dialysis. In those early days, the anti-rejection drugs were such that a twin or a close family member was needed before transplantation would be attempted.

I was considered a good candidate due to new and improved anti-rejection medications along with the fact that I was young (46) and in good health otherwise; I didn't look or feel sick. Just a little tired, but then who wouldn't be, working a full time stressful career in commercial sales and blending a family of five kids (at transplant time their ages were 14, 14, 16, 18, and 22)? In fact, when I checked in at the clinic the first time, I was asked if I was the donor!

This brings up the most important step for me–finding a donor. In 2001 there were 3 available treatments for kidney disease: (1) find a deceased donor, (2) find a living donor, or (3) dialysis. Dialysis was my last alternative because, although dialysis is a means of staying alive, it causes the body to deteriorate and age much faster. The deceased donor list was a viable option but that list was long (currently over 100,000 on the waiting list). Finding a living donor became my preferred solution because both donors and recipients can typically live normally with one kidney and the recipient can usually find a living donor quicker than waiting for a deceased donor, minimizing the wait time during which he or she would become sicker.

The time had come for me to find a living donor. The transplant staff asked me if I knew anyone. You must understand, I am a Minnesotan, Lutheran, and Scandinavian who does not want to ask anyone for a dime! How could I ask someone for an internal organ they are physically using so I could have it? I have a difficult time accepting lunch from someone, much less a kidney! In fact, I felt that I would rather die than ask anyone to be cut open for me! The reality was I would die if I didn't' ask, which became quite an incentive to do so.

How does one ask for a kidney before social media? It helped to be born to a mom like mine who began spreading the word for me. In 2001, the majority of transplants were still family members. A few family members stepped up to be tested. My brother was a 6 out of 6 perfect match, but with our family history a perfect match was not necessarily a good thing. My husband, Tom, was also tested. Although the numbers were not quite as compatible as my brother's were, he was deemed the best match. **(LIFE LESSON: ASK FOR WHAT YOU NEED.)**

Five

BLENDING

Tom and I had been married and combining a family of five kids for seven years. Yet on October 22, 2001 we became truly blended.

The morning of the transplant, my mom, middle stepson Paul, Tom, and I went to the HCMC surgical center for the lifesaving exchange. The rest of the family was to follow. Tom and I were prepped and then it was time for surgery. I will always remember Tom walking down the hall in his hospital gown on his way to surgery, knowing that whatever happened in the next few hours, he was doing it for me.

This amazing man, my husband, stepfather to my two girls, and father to his three sons, modeled what love and marriage was all about. "In sickness and in health" was taken to a new level, literally. He was my superhero.

I anxiously waited to be taken in for my surgery, as I worried how Tom was doing in his. Nurses kept me informed periodically until my time drew near and I was given the "before surgery happy juice." When that happened I wasn't bothered in the least with what was happening to Tom or me. I remember telling my surgeon in the pre-op physical to make sure I was asleep during the transplant because I had seen an Oprah show where patients in surgery could hear and feel things going on during their procedures. Thankfully, Tom and I had no problems with that! We both slept through the whole thing!

Tom's pre-op physical and evaluation was quite different from mine. He tried to get his surgeon to agree that his kidney donation to me warranted sex-on-demand for the rest of his life! I believe his surgeon pleaded the fifth. I told Tom that because his surgery was being done laparoscopically (Tom was one of the first in Minnesota to have the small incision, minimal invasion kidney removal surgery that has now become the standard) not to count on it! On the other hand, I tried to figure out how many times I would have to wash his underwear, clean up after him, and/or fix his dinners before I could possibly be able to pay him back. Living with the realization that I could never do so was tough. **(LIFE LESSON: ACCEPT THE GIFT GRACIOUSLY, NO PAYBACKS NECESSARY.)**

Our family waited together and cheered when they were informed that Tom's very LARGE kidney (emphasis on large) was walked into my surgical room next door, inserted in me, and began to make urine right away. Just so there is no confusion, the recipient's surgery is much more invasive than the donor's, who is able to have a laparoscopic procedure. My natural kidneys were left in place, and a large incision was made on the left side of my belly/pelvis area. The new kidney was inserted just underneath my pelvis, and hooked up directly to my bladder. (Just the place you want a very LARGE kidney!) Although I was now lopsided and knew my bikini days were over, Tom's kidney had made a new home in my body, it was working, and it appeared to be happy there, which is what we were going for!

I was wheeled from recovery to my room in somewhat of a daze. I remember my family surrounding me and telling me my color was so good and I looked like a million bucks. Little did they know I felt like I had been hit by a Mack truck! Having had surgery only once before in my life (tonsillectomy), I was unprepared. Apparently, I was doing much better than Tom who was lying in his room green and nauseated from the pain meds.

Truly blended.

Six

Drugs, Drugs and Lack Thereof

A thick three-ring binder was handed to me prior to the transplant, describing each anti-rejection medication, what it did, and what the side effects were. It was overwhelming! I tried to get through the book but finally slammed it shut. I made the decision I would worry about the side effects if or when they happened. In the hospital, right after transplant, I began a regimen of 70 pills a day. Each pill I took was designed to keep my body functioning, while tricking it into thinking Tom's LARGE kidney belonged inside of me. I was fortunate that I was taking no meds prior to the transplant. I was nauseous constantly. Therefore, food did not initially appeal to me. My body not only had to adjust to taking all of the new meds, but I had to learn how and when to take each one. I had never seen such a large pillbox! The nurses in the hospital taught me how to fill each compartment by morning, noon, and evening dosages.

The anti-rejection meds require time-sensitive dosages, so I learned to set alarms so I would not forget or be late. I did everything the doctors told me to do, as I did not want to reject Tom's kidney. The follow-up clinic appointments were set in place. Initially I began getting rides the 20 or so miles to downtown Minneapolis three days a week to the clinic where I would receive blood draws and checkups. I was monitored continually to watch for any signs of rejection or infection. Eventually my checkups were weaned from three times a week to two, from once a week to every other week, and eventually to once a month. For the first year after transplant, I was tethered to HCMC.

Living immunosuppressed begins a new way of life. My family was asked to sanitize the doorknobs, refrigerator door handles, countertops, etc. in my own home before I got back so I would not be exposed to additional germs. I was also encouraged to stay away from large crowds. After six weeks of healing at home, I was able to go back to work and into the reality of a world full of nasty germs. Hand sanitizer was in my purse at all times. I had to stay away from coughing and sneezing people, which is not easy when you also have school age kids. I became aware of things like touching anything at a mall, or exercise equipment at the club, or even shaking hands during the welcome at church. Living in Minnesota was a blessing as it gave me the opportunity to wear gloves; I just had to remember not to put them up to my eyes or face.

Six months after transplant I began to run a fever. It continued to get higher with no apparent flu or cold symptoms. After a visit to the transplant clinic, I was put back in the hospital to find the underlying cause.

It was horrible timing for me as my employer was in the middle of doing a massive reorganization and all sales people were required to attend a weeklong conference at the home office in Wisconsin. It was extremely important that I be there to, in addition to everything else, find out what my new territory would be. Instead, I was lying, feverish, in a hospital bed talking on a cell phone, distressed about what I was missing.

I remember a nurse giving me a reality check when she came into the room and saw me on the phone. "Linda! THIS IS YOUR LIFE." Until that moment, I really did not realize that any little fever or flu was a big deal for a transplant patient. I had gone to work at the office on a Friday, had a kidney transplant on Monday, and was back to work six weeks later, just like having a baby, so I thought! I learned at that hospital stay that post-transplant sickness is different from pre-transplant sickness.

As it turned out, the fever was due to fluid that had collected around my new kidney surgery area. I had to wear a drain for a week or so, but once that fluid was drained my fever was gone. I was fortunate the fluid was not infected.

I began to realize that things were different now. I was given a gift, extended life, and did not want to waste it. I asked Tom to make a list with me of things we wanted to do, places we wanted to see, and people with whom we wanted to spend time. It forced us to look at what, and whom, was important to us. We had celebrated Christmas with my in-laws, Wally and Arlene, and were driving home. Tom drove as I wrote our New Year's bucket list. We kept the list on his dresser and began to check items off as precious time ticked by. **(LIFE LESSON: PRIORITIZE WHAT'S MOST IMPORTANT AND DO IT.)**

A few months into the transplant, I began to "look" like I was on prednisone. This was not a surprise, as I was on a massive dose for a long period. I gained weight–40-50 pounds, and my face was puffy and round. I was quite embarrassed about the way I looked. My oldest stepson, Mark, got married at the peak of my marshmallow face, Frankenstein/hulk body. I am surprised I did not scare off our daughter-in-law Nicole! Finding a stepmother of the groom's dress was a real treat. I bought a black dress with a velvet tent-like jacket to wear over it. Our friends and family at the wedding barely recognized me. I did not even recognize myself! I remember putting lotion on my legs after a shower and wondering to whom did these legs belong!

I also found it difficult to make sales calls to my clients at work. Business owners did not know who I was and it was obvious something wasn't right. I worried that clients who noticed I was "sick" would wonder if I would be able to take care of their accounts. Selling new accounts was my greatest challenge, although, by the grace of God, I sold the largest non-national account our company had had in years while I was on the prednisone puff. I am certain the buying business owners didn't care what my weight was or how round my face was. They bought because of what I was providing them. Yet I still wanted to scream, "I don't look like this!" **(LIFE LESSON: THE OUTSIDE MAY LOOK DIFFERENT BUT I AM STILL ME.)**

Contrary to some people's belief, prednisone weight is not water weight. Prednisone is a steroid that actually builds tissue. I remember my stepson, Paul, being upset with his girlfriend, Angie, when they were in college. I told him to give me the word and I would sit on her. (For the record, I could have "taken her," but fortunately I did not have to. They made up, got married, and have given us a beautiful grandson all on their own (LOL).

This brings up another characteristic of the lifesaving drug–my emotional fuse was very short. One day I overheard my two daughters talking to a friend of theirs whose mom was also on prednisone. He was warning them about the "look" that would come into his mom's eyes. My kids learned quickly that when my eyes shot out lightning bolts it was best to leave well enough alone. I think they realized that I could "take them" as well and it was best not to push. Most of the time I could control my emotions, but I do remember running down the hall with a rolled-up newspaper after my youngest, Rachel, one evening. I have no recollection what possessed me to do so but it was fortunate she got away long enough for me to settle down and talk rationally. On the other hand, let us just say I talked as rationally as I could on prednisone. **(LIFE LESSON: WHAT SEEMS SANE TO ME ON STEROIDS MAY NOT BE!)**

As I was being weaned off some of my medications I became depressed. I recall women on an episode of the Oprah show sharing their stories about coming down off their prescription drug addictions. I felt the same way they described! The steroids that had zipped me up enough to lose sleep were now being tapered down in my body. I remember needing to pull my company car over in a fast food parking lot so I could call my nurse at the transplant clinic and cry. I felt like I could not function. A week or two later I took a disability leave.

After going back to work for two years and being on disability for an extended length of time, I realized it was not worth my mental health or the second chance of life I had been given to return to my stressful career. I had a choice to make. I could spend my time and energy working at a job that would slowly take my physical and mental health away or find a less stressful career. No amount of money was worth my health. I needed to move on. **(LIFE LESSON: LIFE IS TOO SHORT! BE CAREFUL HOW YOU SPEND IT.)**

Thus began my education in the field of Life Coaching. I went to school to get my life coaching certification and continued on to get my master certification. During this time, The University of Minnesota began a study for transplant recipients on the care of their chronic condition. I participated in the study, which included monitoring the effects of yoga, meditation, and a weekly class on transplant care. I eventually became a facilitator. This experience was eye-opening for me. Participants in the class had not only received kidneys, but also other organs such as livers, hearts, and lungs.

I was shocked when one woman explained to me that she was a living heart donor. Apparently In the early days of lung transplants, the heart could not be separated from the lungs. The whole heart/lung section needed to be removed from the donor. Although her heart was perfectly fine, it had to be removed to make room for the new heart/lung combination that she needed. Her perfectly healthy heart went to someone else in need.

All of us were walking miracles! Each one of us had a unique individual story of how she/he had become part of that elite class, but the one common ground we all stood on was the fact that every one of us had been given a second chance at life. **(LIFE LESSON: APPRECIATE SECOND CHANCES; WE MAY NOT GET A THIRD.)**

As my prednisone amount leveled out, I was given permission to begin a Weight Watchers program, an exercise class at the Y, and a daily walking routine (just like my mom who walked at least a mile daily with her neighbors before it was an exercise "thing"). I began to look and feel like my old normal. I was still living immune-suppressed with someone else's kidney in me, but I had graduated to monthly lab appointments and yearly physicals with the transplant clinic. After weeks, months, and then six years of stable labs, I expected that all would be well. Then one day it wasn't.

Prednisone Puff

Seven

REJECTION

I was in the kitchen making dinner when the phone rang. Doctor Somerville was calling to ask if I was feeling ok. I had just had my labs done and something didn't seem quite right. I went back to the clinic to get a recheck and ultimately back to the transplant clinic for a biopsy. It was 2007 and my oldest daughter, Megan, was in the process of moving to Houston, Texas to student teach. I was excited about Megan's new opportunity but a little concerned as well. She was also under the care of Dr. Somerville.

Four years prior (2003) Megan had gone in for her yearly physical and it was noted that her creatinine was a little high. I had asked our doctor to be on the lookout for any change in both of my daughters' kidney function because of my dad and me. When her creatinine level appeared somewhat high, her doctor did not hesitate to refer her to Dr. Somerville too. He was taking her labs every six months, and although nothing had been diagnosed, I was still a little nervous. **(LIFE LESSON: BE PROACTIVE.)**

Because of the biopsy, I could not fly or lift a box. The kidney is a vascular organ, and my doctor was concerned about me bleeding or getting blood clots on the long cross-country drive. After persisting that

I Need a kidney: Now what?

I wanted to be a part of her move, I was given permission to fly if I promised I would not lift a thing. Megan and her dad had just left with a packed car and I was sitting out on the front steps with tears rolling down my face having just said good-bye.

The phone rang. I could see on the caller ID it was the transplant clinic.

They had my biopsy results.

I was rejecting.

My heart stopped, I closed my eyes, took a very deep breath and asked, "Does that mean I will need another kidney?"

"Yes."

How long?

"Maybe 10 years."

Just like that, my life reverted to the days of living with my kidneys dying.

My alligator tears became sobs! I had done everything I was told. I had taken every precaution to not be around sick people, I used hand sanitizer frequently, I took my pills on time, and I exercised, watched my diet, and had even lost 65 pounds, which was a feat in itself. How could I be rejecting? How was I going to tell Tom?? The gift that he had given me so generously and selflessly was no longer welcome in my body. Somehow, it had figured out that Tom's kidney did not belong there. I was in chronic rejection and heartbroken. I had to keep living knowing that my kidney was dying.

I called Tom with the news. He said he would give me his other kidney. **(LIFE LESSON: THERE ARE NO GUARANTEES.)**

Eight

S#*T

Waiting for total kidney failure this time was different from the last. This time the rest of my health deteriorated along with my kidneys. It began with a cold and upper respiratory infection. I was prescribed an antibiotic to take care of the infection, and a couple of weeks later I contracted diarrhea. It persisted and a stool sample was ordered. The diagnosis was Clostridium diff or CDiff. As I understand it, common antibiotics can kill the good bacteria in our colon and bad bacteria begins to overtake it. It is a life threatening condition, not to mention gross. I was nauseous and had diarrhea constantly. The irony about treating CDiff is it requires a very large dose of another very potent antibiotic to cure. The problem I had with CDiff is that I never got rid of it. I was prescribed the dose of the potent drug and inevitably, CDiff would return. The extremely unfortunate part of that was I never knew when I would get it back.

For example, Tom and I were on a trip in Rhode Island for his work and we took his client to dinner. The smell of the fish made me nauseous. I wound up in the bathroom sitting on the toilet with a wastepaper basket on my lap doing you know what from both ends! Another time Tom and I were in Maui and I ran to the bathroom. This time there was no wastepaper basket and paper towel had to suffice. You can only imagine!

I will spare you any more gory details but I suffered from this nasty condition for two years. My weight dropped to 102 pounds. I looked like a skeleton! By this time, I was seeing a gastroenterologist. After a colonoscopy, he discovered I had CMV, which is another nasty infection that transplant recipients in particular can get. Another new drug for my other new, infectious disease doctor to coordinate. Would it never end?

Finally, my gastro doctor referred me to yet another gastro doctor who, as fate would have it, was local, on staff at the University of Minnesota, and, doing a study on what I call poop transplants. Can you believe it? I could not be added to the national kidney transplant list due to my CDiff infection, and in order to correct CDiff I needed to get a poop transplant! Apparently, the study was showing a high success rate by taking a donor's healthy stool and inserting it into an unhealthy colon for the purpose of regenerating good bacteria in the colon and overcoming the bad.

You can only imagine my horror thinking I would have to ask someone to donate his or her poop to me! Tom had been feeling left out and was looking for something to donate to me again so he volunteered right away. We determined this would be the perfect job for him as he was full of s#*t. We drove to that appointment prepared with a willing donor. Unbeknownst to us, the doctor informed us they already had approved donors on a list so it was not necessary for me to find my own.

After reviewing my case, the doctor was reluctant to do the poop transplant. As a transplant patient the fact that I would be able to keep off of antibiotics for any length of time was a crap shoot (so to speak) and as this was important to the transplant study I was s#*t out of luck (literally)! Another part of the study involved "clean environments." We were told to sanitize our home with bleach, cleaning doorknobs, sinks, toilets, carpets, etc. to prevent re-infecting myself. We hoped the sanitization would stop the infection. Fortunately, Tom was working with a company that had a cleaning agent (Decon7) used in cleaning military housing that was proven to clear up everything from mold to MRSA and CDiff. He cleaned the carpets with it, wiped everything down, and fogged our entire house. To date I have never had CDiff again. **(LIFE LESSON: WHEN S#*T HAPPENS, FIND A WAY TO CLEAN IT UP.)**

Nine

Toward the end of the life of my (Tom's) kidney, the respiratory problems I had experienced earlier recurred. The lung specialist I was seeing diagnosed me with pneumonia. I was prescribed a medication to cure the pneumonia along with another heavy duty med to safeguard me from CDiff. I was keeping my infectious disease doctor and the pharmacist in business. Unfortunately, Dr. Somerville had the daunting task of quarterbacking all of the specialists I was seeing in addition to monitoring my kidney deterioration as well.

Somewhat prior to this, after three years in Houston Megan moved back to Minnesota. I was more than pleased and somewhat relieved to have her back home. She too was still under the care of Dr. Somerville who noticed her creatinine trend was rising and determined she needed a kidney biopsy.

The kidney tissue from the biopsy was taken to the same person who analyzed mine at HCMC. For the first time in all of the years of kidney disease in our family we were given a name for what plagued us--Medullary Cystic Disease. Apparently this is an extremely rare genetic disease that affects the kidney filters and very little is known about it. We were devastated that Megan had the same thing I did, but pleased

27

there was a name to attach to it and not one they would have to assign my dad's name to, if you know what I mean. Megan began her wait alongside me as Dr. Somerville led our way. **(LIFE LESSON: WHEN YOU HAVE A NAME FOR THE PROBLEM, YOU CAN BEGIN TO FIND ANSWERS.)**

Ten

CONNECT

In the past, I was married to an ELCA Lutheran Pastor, the father of my two daughters, Megan and Rachel. Because of that experience I have a special place in my heart for clergy families, particularly clergy spouses. A friend invited me to serve on a committee at our church, Prince of Peace, where we had recently hired a new lead pastor, Jeff Marian. As fate would have it, his wife Nancy, was on the committee too. We became fast friends. Nancy and two out of her three boys suffered from an uncommon pancreatic disease that eventually leads to cancer.

They too were visiting doctors regularly for checkups and scans. We shared the "mommy guilt" that washed over us at times, thinking our kids shared our genes, therefore if they develop the same condition it is our fault. Yet, I have always known that if I accepted responsibility for that, I would have to blame Dad too. Was it God's fault? Although Nancy and I never (that I recall) blamed it on God, I am sure she pondered the same question I did.

At least I knew another mother who shared a common situation. Tom and I became close to Jeff as well. We grilled out together, shared rotary events together, and went out to dinner many times. It was at one of those dinners we shared my situation with Jeff. Tom's kidney was failing and I would someday soon need a donor. Immediately Jeff offered to give me his. My eyes brimmed with tears just knowing he had offered. I told him thanks for even considering the idea and left it at that.

He told me later that he had felt a tug. Shortly after our dinner, he approached me at a Bible study asking for the phone number to the transplant clinic. Next thing I knew he told me he had made the decision to pursue donating. I had been living with Tom's kidney the past 12 years and had been informed that 97% of the population would not match me due to the buildup of so many antibodies. At that time I had been taken off the national transplant list because I was not healthy enough to be a recipient. Still, Jeff took the step forward to become a lifesaver. **(LIFE LESSON: BECAUSE OF YOUR PAST, YOU HAVE A FUTURE.)**

Eleven

HEARTBROKEN

It was the end of the summer of 2012 and I noticed I was extremely out of breath after trying to walk up a flight of stairs, and I still had a nagging cough. I figured it was pneumonia again. I thought I better get it checked out. I called Dr. Somerville and ran in to my local clinic for a chest x-ray. The good news was I did not have pneumonia. The bad news was I was in heart failure and ordered to the hospital immediately! I was flabbergasted to say the least. The clinic doctor told me it warranted going to the hospital by ambulance immediately. I had just left my house to run to the clinic. Tom was working out of our home, but I didn't want him to hear the news I had for him by phone. I begged the doctor to allow me to drive home and tell Tom in person and then he could drive me directly to the hospital. She conceded.

I drove home faster than the speed limit and could feel my heart beating faster than I was driving. I was out of breath, and could not catch a deep one. Tom dropped everything on his desk and quickly drove us to a local hospital where they were waiting for me. I was taken directly to the ER and hooked up to more than one monitor. After a number of tests, I was told I needed to spend the night. How could this be? I was totally stunned! One organ failure was enough! This was the lowest I had felt since I was diagnosed with kidney failure the first time, or maybe the second time, I am not sure which was worse. Anyway, I was informed that fluids in my body that the kidney was unable to dispose of were beginning to back up and my heart was having a tough time pumping up to expectations. I spent the night at the hospital being watched, monitored, tested, and scanned.

In the morning it was determined I needed to be brought by ambulance to a different hospital. My heart was only working at 30% capacity and there was a good chance I would need a pacemaker. ARE YOU KIDDING ME!?!?!? Things were happening so fast I barely knew which end was up. First, I thought, I JUST had pneumonia! I was having a hard time wrapping my head around the fact I was now in congestive heart failure. Second, I was transported by ambulance to a hospital other than HCMC, and third, Dr. Somerville was on vacation. As I was transported to the new hospital I began to lose hope. For the first time I realized I was really, really sick.

I was admitted to that hospital until the drugs they administered were able to get rid of the fluids my kidneys could not. I was hooked up to an IV diuretic, and as the fluid dispersed, my breathing became better.

During that stay, I had a visit from my dear friends Peter and Karen. They are a clergy couple I had known since I was married to Paul, my former husband. The moment they arrived I got a phone call from my own pastor, Jeff. I remember teasing Jeff that they were trying to recruit me back to their church. Peter and Karen brought me a prayer shawl one of the women from Lord of Life had made, and I never took it off. When Paul and his now-wife, Porat, stopped by, I began to feel uneasy about all the clergy visits. Was this a foretaste of the feast to come? Were they there to see if I needed last rites soon? It became apparent to me that people other than my family thought I was in real trouble. Thankfully, after a week I was discharged with an appointment to see a heart doctor in six months, unless I had symptoms. Until then stay away from salt.

I Need a kidney: Now what?

I was not able to wait six months. Four months later, the week after Christmas, I was having a terrible time breathing again. I sat in a recliner all night because lying down was awful! I phoned the heart doctor on call, and after our conversation she instructed me to get to the ER if I got any worse.

An hour or two later I was downstairs watching a movie with Tom. He was planning to go out to walk our dog in the sunny cold January air. I got up from the chair to go to the bathroom and could not make it back. I got a far as the footstool and collapsed over it panting, struggling to catch my breath! By the grace of God, Tom came back downstairs to get something he had forgotten. He saw me sprawled out over the footstool and whispering, "I don't like this." He picked me up and carried me up the flight of stairs to the front door. Tom grabbed our coats and my prayer shawl and placed me in the car to speed the few minutes to our neighboring hospital. We considered going to my heart hospital but we knew I did not have time. I hung my head out the window in the cold air thinking it would help me get more air. **(LIFE LESSON: IT'S OK TO CALL AN AMBULANCE, IT'S OK TO ASK FOR HELP.)**

Minutes later, we squealed into the ER entrance. I was wheel-chaired in immediately and given a room. A forced-air mask was placed over my face to get me the needed oxygen. I was finally able breathe, which helped me to relax.

The next morning was Sunday. Our church, Prince of Peace, is across the street from the hospital. Tom shared our more-than-exciting evening, and a few friends walked across the street to see me. Pastor Jeff and Nancy were part of the pack. By this time people were beginning to realize I needed a kidney sooner rather than later. A number of friends approached Tom and I to ask questions about becoming a donor. Some went so far as to ask about being tested. Meanwhile, Jeff was beginning to wonder if a transplant would even be possible

This hospital stay was much like the previous one. Diuretics, diuretics, diuretics. The best news for me was Dr. Somerville was in the house.

I remember the heart doctor asking me health questions. All I had to say was "ask Dr. Somerville." Later that day the doctor came in for rounds and told me he had received the information he needed. In addition, he said, "That guy knows everything about you." **(LIFE LESSON: GET A GOOD DOCTOR YOU TRUST AND DEVELOP A RELATIONSHIP.)**

Twelve

SALT

I was instructed to be on a very low sodium diet when I was sent home from the hospital. Tom became the salt sergeant In hopes of keeping me out of the hospital again; and I did not want to struggle breathing ever again, so I followed every instruction to a T. Tom read every label of anything we ate to monitor salt grams. Our diet became mostly fresh food, which is not an easy feat in our Minnesota winters. Bread and soup, a previous mainstay all winter long, was a no-no due to the overload of salt. Tom learned how to make homemade soup with minimal salt. He also brought out the bread machine, which had not used since the Minnesota Twins won the World Series in 1991! My favorite was when he experimented with making a low sodium pizza crust in the bread maker. Fresh veggies on top with a homemade pizza sauce, and I could finally eat pizza again!

All the while Tom cooked and counted sodium I made friends with NCIS (all of them), Hawaii Five-0, Blue Bloods, and Hallmark movies. I also knit like a fiend. This was a great hobby to acquire in the winter. Scarves, mittens, headbands, and shawls. I made them all. I appreciated even more the prayer shawl Peter and Karen brought me in the hospital.

By the spring of 2013 my heart failure was under control. I weighed in every morning and called in the results to the heart clinic so they could keep track of any fluid retention. I was up and around more and feeling a bit hopeful that I was finally coming out of the woods. Then I began to run a fever.

Thirteen

ENOUGH IS ENOUGH

I remember calling Dr. Somerville's office while I was still in bed under the covers. I told my nurse how awful I felt and that I had a fever. Dr. Somerville was doing rounds at my neighborhood hospital and his nurse told me she would call him right away. I told her to tell him that I did not want to get out of bed and maybe he could prescribe me something over the phone. She called back shortly and told me to get to the ER. It was a God-thing that Tom was working out of the house that morning. I quickly got dressed, brushed my teeth, and grabbed my prayer shawl. "Here we go again."

Tom drove and Dr. Somerville met us in the ER. More tests, scans, and bloodwork. I was so tired. It was confirmed that I not only had kidney and heart failure, but three different infections, and possibly cancer. I refused to have cancer too. I remember telling the oncologist that came into my room, in no uncertain terms, that I did not have cancer. Thankfully, I didn't!

By this time our kids were out of college and more or less on their own. Mark was married with three young kids, Paul was married, Megan was recently engaged and planning her wedding and John and Rachel were starting new careers.

Megan and her future husband, Charlie, came to see me in the hospital, sharing stories about their pre-marital classes. Their wedding was only 10 weeks away. I was wondering if I would make it.

Rachel's birthday was April 22 and we had planned to take her to dinner. Instead, I was lying in the hospital bed. Family came to visit me first, and then they left for the restaurant. While I was looking out the window at the swirling snow, thinking life was passing me by, I realized in that hospital bed that I was not in control of one thing. This could be it, the end of the road. There was nothing else I could do. I made the decision to let go and let God. A peace and calmness washed over me. Whatever happened, I knew I would be ok and my family would be ok.

Do not get me wrong. Letting go is not giving up. I did not want Megan to be without her mom at her wedding. I wanted to see whom John and Rachel would choose as their life partners. I wanted to see the grandkids grow up and hoped I would enjoy more grandkids. I wanted to live. On the other hand, more than anything, I wanted to have a healthy life. I woke up in a panic attack one night thinking I could not do another transplant. By this time I knew too much. It was not like replacing a car part! A part of me was ready to be finished with all the drugs and all of the sickness. Yet, at that moment I felt that either way, whatever happened, in the end it would turn out ok. I finally felt at peace. **(LIFE LESSON: IN THE END GOD ALWAYS WINS.)**

Fourteen

MIRACLES HAPPEN

It was nothing short of miracle when the doctors were able to clear up all three infections. I still had kidney and heart failure but somehow I was able to walk out of that hospital on two wobbly legs. I was so weak initially; I had a hard time walking from my bedroom to the kitchen. Thankfully, my sisters, Sue and Carrie, took some time out of their busy lives and their jobs to get me back on my feet. My 80 -something mom was also on the list to babysit me. I became stronger every day. Megan's wedding was approaching, and I was home to be a part of it all. I began to consider the fact I may not be done yet. Maybe our living God had more in mind for me. I was just beginning to find out.

The morning of Megan's wedding, Jeff texted me: "another reason to celebrate, I've been approved as a donor!" After a number of months doing blood tests, scans, and psychological testing, the waiting stopped. We knew the answer. Jeff was approved! Donors need to be in excellent health (check), they must have a blood type that matches the recipient, (Jeff's was a universal blood type–check), and they have to be psychologically sound (questionable with Jeff but apparently good enough to be accepted (LOL)). Megan's wedding became the pinnacle of celebrations. My family welcomed Jeff as one of our own, my brother from another mother! We were on our way.

Shortly after the wedding cross matches of Jeff's and my blood were done. It was a huge disappointment, but not a surprise, when our test results came back not a match. The antibodies I had built up in my blood would fight his kidney. This test was not even available when Tom and I were going through the process. I was happy science had progressed so far, but much more fearful, feeling I would never find a match knowing the odds were less than 1%.

Living Large at Megan's Wedding

Fifteen

Paired Exchange

After my first transplant, my entire family became more aware of their creatinine levels. My youngest sister had been monitoring hers, and shortly after my transplant she asked me to have Dr. Somerville send my file to her doctors in Madison. They had been watching her for nearly ten years when they determined it was transplant time. She had been advised that 99% of the population would not match her. Sue began the wait.

It was 4:00 am in the morning when Tom and I received a call from Sue. There was a potential deceased donor match for her at the transplant clinic in University of Wisconsin so she called Tom and I for input. It made sense to me that when 99% of the population is not going to match, you GO. Sue and my brother-in-law, Andy, drove the hour ride to Madison. She was prepped for surgery, but when the blood work and everything else was done, the kidney was not a good enough match. Sue and Andy returned home that next evening emotionally and physically exhausted.

In December of 2010 Sue became part of the paired exchange program. The paired exchange program was designed to shorten the time that a patient had to wait for a kidney. Those patients who have a living donor with whom they are not compatible are paired with another couple in the same position so that donors could be exchanged and both patients receive a transplant. There are different kinds of donor recipient chains. Some are straightforward swaps, "paired exchange," some involve multiple donor-patient pairs, "closed chain," and some involve a non-directed anonymous donor and a person on the waitlist, "domino-chain."

One of my college friends called me a couple of years into my first transplant. She wanted to know how my kidney was working because she felt led to donate hers and she didn't know of anyone in need. Sharon ended up becoming one of the first anonymous donors. I went to see her the day after her surgery. She shared with me that as she had walked across the hospital campus that morning the hardest part for her was not having a picture in her mind of who she was donating to. After surgery she found a bouquet of roses next to her bedside, along with a card. On the cover of the card was a picture of seven or eight young children. Inside the card was the note: "Thank you for saving our grandpa."

Sixteen

A Miracle and a Half

Although I was quite aware of the paired exchange program, I did not want to push the idea with Jeff. I felt that Jeff had a way out, now that we knew he and I were not a match. Jeff told me one of his sons asked him if he was relieved or disappointed. He responded he was somewhat disappointed. My sister, Sue, and I have such a hard time understanding the amazing heart of a donor. Both of us have shared that we did not think we would have been able to donate an organ and we are more than grateful that there are people who are so willing and self-sacrificial to do so.

The transplant staff approached Jeff about the paired exchange program. Jeff was not bothered by the fact that I would not be the actual recipient of his kidney. He told me once they removed his kidney he did not care what happened to it. I was the face of whom he was doing it for, as he was the face of my donor as well. He said yes to the paired exchange program.

I had been warned that even on the paired exchange list it would most likely take a year or two to find a match because of my problem antibodies. In the meantime, my condition continued to deteriorate and Dr. Somerville had me see a surgeon to have a shunt put in my arm for dialysis. The reality began to set in; Tom's kidney was nearly gone and I, like my father before me, would be living life on a machine.

It was a Saturday afternoon and our friends, David and Dawn, dropped by. We talked about my situation, that I had a donor that did not match me, and even though we were going to be added to the paired exchange list, it would take a year or two to find a match. Therefore, I had surgery scheduled in a few days to have the shunt put in for dialysis. Dave looked at me and said, "miracles happen." I told him I believed in miracles and had seen a number of them, BUT it would have to be a miracle-and-a-half for me to avoid that shunt surgery in 6 days. He responded, "NEVER underestimate the power of God."

Our names were added to the paired exchange list on Tuesday. Our first match run was Wednesday. The next day, Thursday, a match showed up! By the Grace of God I was able to cancel the shunt scheduled for Friday. **(LIFE LESSON: NEVER UNDERESTIMATE THE POWER OF GOD, AND I MEAN NEVER!)**

The next step in the process was to confirm by blood test cross matches what the papers on the paired exchange list showed. It looked like it could be a true-paired exchange. In other words, a donor who matched me was giving to a recipient who would match Jeff–a true-paired exchange. Cross matches needed to be done to confirm. A brief wait and more blood and we would know for sure if what the paperwork showed held true. IT DID!

I woke up to our phone ringing around 3:00 in the morning. When the phone rings at that time of night it can never be good. I was afraid to answer it, afraid that it had something to do with one of our kids. Caller ID showed the transplant clinic. ARE YOU KIDDING? NOW WHAT! Someone on the other end of the phone explained that a deceased donor had become available and it looked to be a match for me.

I immediately woke up, on full alert, with Tom joining me when I sprung to a sitting position in our bed. My first reaction was that Jeff would not have to do this. He would not have to have surgery or put himself at risk for me. I had minutes to decide. A family had lost a loved one and in their grief had so generously made a choice to share their loved one's organs so others may live. My head was swimming! I took a breath and remembered what my sister had experienced in Madison. Yet I also remembered what I had advised her...you have to GO.

We were having a birthday party that afternoon, just a few hours away. All the kids were coming over to cook out. I couldn't miss that. Another breath. Somewhere in Atlanta, two people unknown to me, unknown to Jeff, were sleeping soundly depending on us. I confirmed with the voice on the other end of the phone that the only thing left on the paired exchange program was to set a date. The response was there are never any guarantees, but for now, yes, all we had to do was set a date. However, what about Jeff? If I accepted the deceased donor kidney he would not have to donate his. Tom looked into my terror-filled eyes and said, "Linda, don't take this away from him." I held my breath, momentarily, then told the transplant clinic to give that kidney to the next person on the list.

In less than five minutes I had decided something that could have rocked not only my life, but also the lives of so many others. Did I do the right thing? Tom and I turned the lights back off and laid back down. He confirmed that I had made a good choice, the right thing. I still was not sure. Someone had died that night. I was told it was an accident. I silently prayed for the deceased donor family, thanking God for the decision they had made to donate. I prayed for the next person on the list, whomever that may be, thinking that maybe they didn't have another opportunity for a kidney, maybe they were on dialysis waiting, maybe they were home sleeping in bed waiting for "the call" hoping one day they would get a second chance. I prayed for the two people in Atlanta hoping everything would work out for them, for us, for all of us. Mostly I prayed for Jeff. Nothing could ever happen to Jeff. Tom was breathing deeply by then. I am not sure I ever slept.

Seventeen

The Exchange

In early fall of 2013 the paired exchange was finalized, which in itself is not an easy task. It is beyond me how two transplant hospitals across the country coordinate all the details. We were fortunate that the pair Jeff and I would soon be exchanging with was in Atlanta, GA, a hub for Delta airlines. In case you were wondering, after a kidney is harvested it is packed up in a cooler, fitted with a tracking device, and flown across the country to its new home. Since Atlanta is a hub for Delta airlines, there were numerous choices for transporting the kidney, which was a blessing (the minimum amount of time an organ is out of the body the better). The date set was October 8, 2013.

Tom and I planned to pick up Jeff and Nancy early in the morning, as we were due into the surgery center at HCMC at 4:30 or 5:00 am. That morning we drove in the darkness to pick up Jeff, Nancy, and our friend and prayer warrior, Marilyn, from church. As we drove downtown to HCMC, I remember telling Jeff that whereas Tom had requested sex-on-demand for the rest of his life when he gave me his kidney, I still for the life of me, had no idea why he would do this for me.

We checked into the pre-op and I hugged Jeff good-bye knowing the next time I saw him he would be missing something. I was led to my own pre-op room where Tom sat with me for a brief few minutes then ran off to find Marilyn, Nancy, and Jeff. I was alone. I could not believe it was here, again. In a few hours, I would have a third chance at life. So many things to worry about. It was hard to imagine there were two other people across the country that were being checked out right along with us. I was hoping and praying there would not be a delayed flight, or that our precious package would not be lost. In the pre-surgery physical I had asked the doctor for some sort of anti-anxiety medication to calm me down the day of the surgery. I thought I would be a nervous wreck waiting for Jeff's surgery to be over. I was fearful that our very large congregation would be angry with me if anything happened to Jeff! Not to mention his wife, and three boys. I would never forgive myself saying no to the call I had at 3:00 am a few weeks ago. I would have guilt for the rest of my life! Everything had to be all right.

Now the day was here, and although I felt butterflies, much as if I would think an athlete feels on game day, I felt amazingly calm. Again, I was in the position where there was nothing I could do. Everything was arranged. We had done our part and now our transplant was in the hands of a very big God, right where it should be.

While Jeff was in surgery, Tom, Nancy, Marilyn, and I found the prayer and meditation room. We paced the meditation-walk pattern on the floor, wrote our private prayers on paper and placed them on the Wailing Wall. Tom and Nancy had set up a Caring Bridge site, which is a site that connects and informs loved ones during health events, so people from our congregation and other friends, and family would be updated on our progress. Our loved ones messaged us with prayers, encouraging words, and well wishes. As the hours ticked by, I became more and more peaceful. I could actually feel a warmth from people praying. I felt like I was wrapped in a cocoon of peace. **(LIFE LESSON: PRAYER WORKS: WHATEVER THE ANSWER, YOU ARE NOT ALONE.)**

The surgeon informed Nancy that it was over and Jeff had done well. Thank God!! Relief flooded my heart. We were halfway there! What happened to me was not nearly as concerning as the fact that Jeff was all right. The gift Jeff had so graciously given revealed exactly who Jeff is. He loves the world and the all the people in it. I made Jeff a special gift and asked Tom to bring it to the hospital the day after our transplant. Earlier that summer I ran across a rock in the shape of a kidney. I spray painted it gold and printed a Bible verse on it: "No greater love has man, than to lay down his life for a friend." I can never repay, never earn what he did, and will never ever forget. It is because of him, I live.

I was paged that my new kidney had landed at Minneapolis-Saint Paul Airport. It was my turn. I was directed to what would be my hospital room as a transport was sent to pick up my new kidney. Tom ran down the hall to do a check of Jeff and I got dressed into my surgical gown as my family waited. Jeff was half-asleep but gave thumbs up to me. One more prayer in my room from our care pastor. My family gathered around along with Nancy and one of their boys and laid hands on me during the prayer. It was time. As I said good-bye to all, I noticed tears in my daughters' eyes as they wheeled me down the hall. Tom walked with me to pre-op. As they were prepping me for surgery, I talked to the doctors attending. Was it a coincidence that we had three Lutheran college graduates (Luther, St. Olaf, and Gustavus, my alma mater) performing and attending my transplant? I think not! It was then I knew I was in REAL good hands and could rest knowing all was well. Ok, well, that happy juice most likely had something to do with it but I was confident in my team. Tom kissed me good-bye with tears in his eyes, and my surgeon was in charge.

Five minutes later, I woke up in a dark room with Tom by my side. Ok, I guess it was five or so hours but to me, well, I slept through the whole thing. I remember asking Tom how I did. "Perfect. " His response made my day, and more importantly my new life. Perfect. Somehow, some unknown person had given up their kidney, which had flown across the country in a cooler, was wedged into me, and by the grace of God started to do its thing right away. It is hard to comprehend such over-all grace. Jeff was sleeping down the hall minus a major organ that had also been flown across the country, and was now cleansing the blood of another anonymous person. All of us were doing well. Perfect.

Eighteen

THE MORNING AFTER

The morning after the transplant surgery, Jeff was able to walk down to my room with the help of his IV pole. I thought it looked like a shepherd hook. There he was, my pastor, friend, brother from another mother, and superhero, walking all the way from his room down the hall to my room, to check on one of his flock. (It was the first time I have had a visit from a clergy wearing a hospital gown!) No words can describe the gratitude I felt, not only for Jeff, but also for two faceless people in Atlanta. Waking up, I imagined them feeling the way we were feeling. The only thing we knew was that they had made it through the surgery and Jeff's kidney was working in someone else. And for that moment, it was enough. All was well!

Jeff's biggest complaint with his hospital stay was the lack of good TV shows. When I could finally venture down to his room I noted he looked content watching Andy Griffith.

I believe I can speak for Jeff when I say that we more than appreciated the prayers and support from Prince of Peace as well as other friends and family. Both Jeff and I felt the warmth and comfort those prayers gave us through not only the surgery but also the hospital stay. We were hoping they could feel it in Atlanta too. All too soon, or should

I say not soon enough, Nancy and one of their sons, Jacob, took Jeff home, a day before me. I was happy he was going home, but my partner was gone, and I felt like something was missing. Indeed, it was Jeff who was missing something and me who had gained not only a new kidney, but also a new life. Forever bonded, grateful for the choice he made.

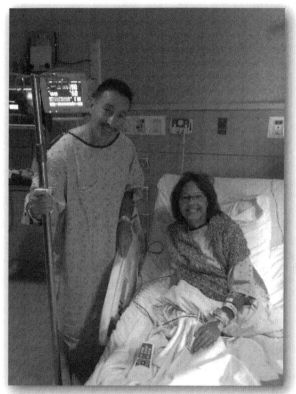

Shepherd Jeff and me in my prayer shawl

Nineteen

The Meeting

A few months after the transplant Jeff and I signed papers to share our personal information with the Atlanta pair in hopes that they would be open to sharing their information and make contact with us. The feeling was mutual so and the four of us signed paperwork to make contact.

I had such a tremendous feeling of gratitude that I needed more than anything to say thank you. I cried as I tried to pen a letter to someone I did not know, yet every time I peed I thought of. It was somewhat strange for me to not personally know the person whose organ I was living with, since the last time I received one I went home to live with my donor. In the meantime, Judy and Jeff had made contact and I heard the story. Tyler, my kidney donor, was donating on behalf of Judy, his mother's best friend. Judy had a universal blood type and shared that her doctor told her that it would be hard to find her a donor because anyone with that blood type would most likely be able to donate to his or her recipient. Judy and Tyler had been waiting on the list for a year. Jeff also had a universal blood type but all the antibodies I had in my blood after living with Tom's kidney 13 years fought Jeff's. Tyler's kidney matched me. Nothing short of a miracle!

I received a letter from Tyler and became Facebook friends with his wife, mother, and Judy. All of us corresponded periodically and I continually asked them to come for a visit. Tyler's mom complied and planned a trip for all of them to come visit us from Atlanta. I was a nervous wreck! I am not sure exactly why. I guess it was weird to think I would finally meet the man who had allowed me to carry his twin kidney. On the other hand, Jeff wasn't fazed in the least. He told me once his kidney left him he didn't really care where it went. Not to say he was not excited when the day arrived that the Atlanta delegation showed up at my door to meet us!

The local news was here filming the whole story! We shared our stories, took pictures, and enjoyed seeing each other in real life. They wanted to visit Prince of Peace and hear Jeff preach, so we went to worship on Saturday evening and enjoyed dinner together afterwards. I will never forget that evening. It was beautiful, four families united forever by a life-changing surgery. I know Judy and I are grateful beyond words for what Jeff and Tyler have done for us. However, Judy said it best when she shared that she was thankful for my illness too. Not that she wanted me to be sick, but if I had not been, Jeff would not have been in the picture to donate to her, and there would have been no Tyler for me.

As time goes on, we continue to keep in touch. Jeff, Nancy, Tom, and I would love to visit them soon, especially when our weather up here starts getting cold! Until then we continue to celebrate our October 8 anniversary apart, yet united! **(LIFE LESSON: NOTHING IS BETTER THAN CONNECTING FACE TO FACE.)**

P.S. in case you are wondering, I still talk Minnesotan without a southern drawl, but unexpectedly have a desire to say "y'all" on rare occasions.

Sister Sue and brother-in-law Andy, with the Atlanta gang

Forever linked Jeff, Judy, Tyler and me

Twenty

What Now?

I am happy to admit I have graduated from living moment-by-moment to day-by-day. The first year after my transplant I walked around waiting for the other shoe to drop. Although I still hold my breath until I get the creatinine level results in my monthly labs, I am much more comfortable thinking things are ok. People continue to ask me what the prognosis is. The truth is I have no idea. There is no crystal ball to foresee what the future will be. If you are fortunate enough to receive a new kidney, it does not come with an expiration date. I have one friend who has had her kidney over 30 years! My first transplant with Tom did not include the antibody tests that Jeff, Judy, Tyler, and I went through. I am hoping this kidney will hold me through the rest of my life, but as we all know, there are never any guarantees.

Medullary Cystic Disease is very rare. Because of that, the answers we long for are not available. We live in the hope of gaining the answers we need, and I am keeping my fingers crossed that it will be soon. My daughter, Megan, and her husband, Charlie, would like to start a family but they know Megan is labeled high-risk because of our disease. My sister and I were fortunate to have already had our children before our kidneys had deteriorated to the point hers are at now.

I Need a kidney: Now what?

A recent study for our Medullary Cystic Disease determined two genes that define our kidney problem. If you have the disease, you carry the genes with the knowledge each child you bear has a 50-50 chance of having the disease. If you do not have the disease, you cannot pass it on. There is no specialty test at the present time that our children could take to see if they are afflicted, which means my youngest daughter, Rachel, or my sister Sue's two kids will go about their business knowing one day it may rear its ugly head. I am hopeful that the stem cell research currently being conducted using one's own DNA to regenerate a new kidney will be advanced enough to offer another path in place of a transplant. This would eliminate the need for anti-rejection drugs, and I am hopeful could mean there would be no need for donors, living or deceased! We could finally grow enough kidneys to go around!

My dearest Megan, (and anyone else experiencing kidney failure) we already know you are part of the "club" Dad and Ernest started so long ago. I am hoping the life lessons I learned as a child and throughout my life are something you can use as part of your story to help you along your way. I know we are just scratching the surface of whatever your journey will require from me as your mom, but I want to remind you that Grandma cared for not only her husband, but also two daughters. I have learned from the best. Charlie, my favorite son-in-law, you have already been Megan's rock and can always make her laugh exactly when she needs to. I love you for it. I am so very thankful for you! Know that when the inevitable happens Tom and I intend to be there for you too.

To my daughter Rachel, I am hopeful that you have not inherited my kidney genes, but my intention is that the life lessons I have learned can be a part of your life as well, bad kidneys or not. Medullary Cystic Disease usually shows itself by age 40. Dad was 36, Sue was around 40, and Megan was only 25 when she had her biopsy. Keep watching your creatinine! Love you!

To Mark, Paul, and John, I know you have no chance of inheriting my genes, but I love you as my own. Just like my kidney, I did not have you at birth but you are part of me now. You have made excellent choices in life partners. Nicole, Angie, and Anna, I hope the life lessons I have learned can be woven into your family life like my prayer shawl that continues to not only warm me but also to help me feel safe. I love y'all.

Then there are the grandchildren. My dad wanted more than anything to have a grandchild before he died. Unfortunately, that dream was not realized. Maybe that is why I have been given an extension on life; to share the lessons I have learned from him and pass them on to you. Ben, Samantha, Emily, and Liam (and the two on their way), I believe that somewhere on the other side of the veil, your great-grandfather is smiling.

What do I know for sure? That nothing is for sure. So I wake up every morning and like Dad said,

THANK THE LORD FOR ANOTHER DAY! (Every moment of it)

Our Family including Mom June 2017

About the Author

Linda Nelson is a two-time kidney transplant recipient living in Apple Valley, Minnesota with her husband, Tom, and their Golden doodle, Bella. In her free time she enjoys taking Bella for walks around the lake, singing in the church choir, serving as social chair of the neighborhood association, and spending time with her kids and grandkids. Nelson is a Master Certified Life Coach focused on work with organ donors, recipients, and families impacted by transplants.

If you are interested in partnering with a life coach to walk with you in your transplant or dialysis journey as a patient or caretaker, please contact Linda at:

lindanelsonga@gmail.com

69404310R00038

Made in the USA
Middletown, DE
06 April 2018